Hexagon

by Ann-Marie Kishel

first step nonfiction

Lerner Publications Company · Minneapolis

I see a hexagon.

This table is a hexagon.

This bolt is a hexagon.

These pencils are hexagons.

This ball has hexagons.

A honeycomb has many hexagons.

Do you see hexagons?